The Implosion of Las Vegas Entertainers

By

L.S. Baker

1stBooks - rev. 4/11/02

This book's dedicated to all of the contemptuous Entertainment Directors, all the stale non-talented musicians and miasmic musical agents that stain the entertainment in Las Vegas.

ACKNOWLEDGMENTS

I would like to acknowledge all the non-working talented musicians, that if were given the chance to perform, would eviscerate the decaying lounge entertainment in Las Vegas.

CONTENTS

PREFACE

I was about to put the finishing touches on this book when America's heart beat experienced a devastating loss of life with the terrorist attacks in New York and Washington D.C. My heart aches painfully for all the victims and their families of this senseless tragedy. America will prevail against terrorism.

The financial future of every business in America has already experienced some form of financial distress and the repercussions of this tragedy will linger for some time. Las Vegas casinos most certainly will feel some financial crunch. All though some casinos have laid-off employees, it is only a temporary situation.

Las Vegas casinos will always remain open for business. The bigwig casino corporations have a mountain full of money. Only a few major casino corporations donated one million dollars to the fire fighters' fund of this tragedy. Hollywood movie stars have donated more money to the victims' families. Las Vegas residents have more patriotism than the money hungry casino executives. The money saturated misers will not even donate a penny to the city of Las Vegas to help better education and feed the homeless.

Sin City lacks business integrity. Every financial scam in the world has an office in Las Vegas. Business scams play a huge role in the entertainment scene. It is all about *politics and money* in Las Vegas.

By the time this book is published, I am very optimistic that Las Vegas will be up and running to full capacity. I hope the United States economy will have regained its financial composure to somewhat of a healthy financial shape. America's way of living will have resumed to some degree of normalcy. Regardless, if America is engaged in war and Afghanistan is the battlefield, people will always want entertainment. Sin City is the number one party town.

Las Vegas will always attract people from all over the world. It is the number one tourist destination. The "Entertainment Capitol of the World" exists solely for the tourists, big gamblers and conventions. Spend! Spend! Spend! Money! Money! Money! People from all backgrounds come to Las Vegas to have a grand old time no matter how much it cost. Almost every business in America and the world holds conventions in Las Vegas. Conventions are a major supply of money for the casinos.

I have written this book to inform the typical tourists, CEOs of big companies, conventioneers and worldwide musicians about the stone cold truth behind the music entertainment in Las Vegas. It is a travesty. I am a musician with the determination to finally reveal the ugly side of this pitiable form of entertainment and the people who represent the music entertainers. The politics in the entertainment scene in Las Vegas inadvertently spills over to the tourists and conventioneers. This book reveals the unsavory characters that represent the majority of entertainers and how they are ripping off all of us, including business conventions, that visit the city of lights.

ONE

INTRODUCTION TO LAS VEGAS ENTERTAINMENT

Las Vegas! When you speak it and it rolls of your lips, it sounds so seductive. This city has everything at your fingertips. The alluring fantasies of winning big money, beautiful showgirls that both sexes' dreams of and the best food money can buy. This quintessential city "has it all."

I am a musician in this sin-filled city. Please, do not get it confused with creme-filled! Las Vegas definitely does not taste like a Krispy Kreme donut! I enjoy living in Las Vegas, but it has a wicked dark side that is not so glamorous. I have the urgency to expose what really goes on behind closed curtains, if you will.

When you visit Las Vegas, you expect to get the best entertainment in the world. Well, why not? You are in "The Entertainment Capitol of The World." Well, do I have news for you! Las Vegas casino executives not only want to take your cash, they are also ripping you off when it comes to music entertainment. This town has more corn in it than Iowa. Could you please pass the salt and butter? You will understand the meaning of this joke as you continue reading.

In the good old days, Vegas entertainment was at it's best. Who can forget the indelible Frank Sinatra and his Rat

1

Pack? The majestic King of Rock and Roll, Elvis Presley, crowned the viva into "Viva Las Vegas." Today, we still have the impressionable Mr. Las Vegas, Wayne Newton.

Back in the old days, Entertainment Directors were privy to good music. The Entertainment Directors today, for lack of better words, are incompetent. They have zero knowledge of the entertainment business. Most of these people are in charge of the Food and Beverage Department of the casinos. How in the heck can they distinguish a "bottle of beer" from a great "entertainment act"? Entertainment Directors have a business scam of accepting kick-back money. The stone cold truth of Las Vegas is *politics and money*. Forget sleeping with the right person to get a job. It is not applicable in this city. It's all about kissing ass and "SHOW ME THE MONEY!"

So who finds the entertainment acts that are in casino lounges? We can thank those wonderful people who call themselves "agents." I call a majority of them thieves. They are in the same category as used car salespersons. They sell lemons. They are laughing all the way to the bank.

This is when the amusement park fun begins for me. Bette Davis once recited in a movie, "Fasten your seat belts, it's going to be a bumpy ride." You might think I am vindictive and bitter towards agents and Entertainment Directors. I have been a victim of these vultures along with many other musicians. It is an insult to my musical intelligence. Unfortunately, I cannot reveal names of casinos, Entertainment Directors, agents, sex and ethnicity of musicians. I do not want to end up in a court of law down the road. I will get satisfaction exposing their scams.

It's a dirty job, but someone has to clean the scum off the toilet.

TWO

ENTERTAINMENT AGENTS

Illustrations by Nick San Pedro © 2001

Certain agents can care less about talent. Talent is not mandatory for an entertainer. Plenty of entertainment acts

4

hide behind canned music. You can compare it to Karaoke. If you decide to stop and to listen to the music entertainment of any casino lounge, it might be fake.

One agent in town is the emperor of booking sequenced bands. Forget talent! If you can fake playing an instrument and singing, you have the job. This day-old stale piece-of-bread agent will even hire musicians with missing teeth. Can anyone recommend a dentist for these poor people? The agent is a genuine con artist. The agent is relentless and can sell ice to an Eskimo. Most Entertainment Directors are snow balled by this master of corn. Most of the time, the agent's bands do not have returned dates. If they do, it is because the agent has kicked back a wad of cash to the Entertainment Directors. I will talk about this Human Bot Fly later. I am eager to talk about the Rolls Royce of slime agents.

Experts say that cockroaches have been around for millions of years. It is impossible to eradicate these tiny creatures from the earth. Las Vegas is home to one of these tiny creatures. I will call this agent CR, short for cockroach. CR has been conducting bad business in this city for several years. CR will contract big corporate conventions at astronomical prices. CR then takes off the top, thousands of dollars and pays the musician pennies. It is legalized robbery at it's finest. Not only is CR ripping off the musicians, but CR is ripping off CEOs and supplying inadequate entertainment for their business conventions.

This method of operation does not stop here. CR is robbing the average casino lounge acts of several thousands of dollars. The slime bucket is raking in the bucks. The dreadful reality is most musicians are privy to this disgusting agent's business tactics. They just do not care. Most musicians are too cowardly to say anything to CR. They have a fear of losing their jobs. Las Vegas has more musicians per square foot then any place in the world. They need to work.

What can musicians do to stop this thieving agent and finally get the money they deserve?

That is the sixty-four million dollar question. Unfortunately, CR has *exclusive contracts* with certain casinos. CR will buy a package deal with the Entertainment Director. It may include four or five bands at a certain price. CR has the check made out to CR's name. This way, the musician has no idea of the amount of the contract.

Let me throw out some numbers. I personally have not seen these contracts, but these numbers are darn close to reality. I have a little insight to casino budgets. I know someone that works in a high position at a casino. CR might contract five bands at fifty thousand dollars. That's ten thousand dollars per band. The bands get four thousand dollars apiece. Do the math. CR just made a cool and easy thirty thousand dollars. CR *loves* to add insult to injury. The disease ridden insect takes out ten to fifteen percent commission on the four thousand dollars. *Ouch!* That hurts! I have a sudden urge to go to the local store and buy a can of Raid!

Most people have a conscious and would not think twice to take people to the financial cleaners. CR possesses no philanthropic qualities what-so-ever. CR is among the aristocracy of harden criminals. It would take me twenty years to write about CR's shady business deals.

This subject is compelling, so I need to share a few more stories. The blood-sucking tic hired a single act to perform at a high profile casino. CR paid the musician a cheap one hundred dollars for the night. Do you have a guess what the wood-chewing termite raked off the top? Give up? The Brown Recluse Spider took a staggering eleven hundred dollars from the entertainer. Do you think CR drinks Dom Perignon Champagne? Keep in mind that this kid-in-a-candy-store represents countless entertainment acts and has them all booked on a rotation schedule. It does not take a rocket scientist to calculate the income this pig brings home in one week alone. It is incomprehensible. I believe CR owns a private bank. You would assume that the musicians of Las Vegas have had enough of being stabbed in the wallet. As I mentioned before, musicians need to work. They need to eat. Bones are better to chew on than to starve.

Illustrations by Nick San Pedro © 2001

The horror stories are never ending with CR. Keep in mind that musicians talk amongst each other and exchange stories.

Here is a story that will make you swallow your drum sticks. Most casinos reserve nights and weeks for an ethnic theme. A casino wanted an average size band for the theme they had scheduled. The piece of art agent replaced the band with a single act. Supposedly, CR paid the act only five hundred dollars and CR pocketed three thousand dollars. Hum? I wonder what kind of car CR drives? Do you think CR wears designer clothes?

Out of something bad, something good happens. A rumor on the streets has it that two major casinos fired CR, and CR's acts cannot perform at those properties. It does not take long for a cockroach to infest a new dwelling. Somehow, CR gets though the cracks and takes up shop in other casinos. Unfortunately, CR will kick back the Entertainment Directors a fistful of dollars to have CR's acts perform at their casinos. Does *that* sound familiar? Well, guess what? CR and MC, short for master of corn, are partners in crime. These two idiots also book circus acts, celebrity look-a-likes, tribute bands, impersonators and what ever they can get their sticky hands on to make money. I will continue the saga of this circus side show later on down the road.

Most of the musical agents in Vegas are musicians. Most of these scum buckets performed in the casino lounges years ago. CR and MC are still performing with their corn-oil band. Of course, they get all the premium corporate gigs that pay exorbitant amount of green bills. MC's life long dream is to imitate CR's criminal life. MC is probably waiting around for the day CR expires and meets the superior cockroach in the sky. MC would then step in and take over as the boss of Cockroach Productions. MC and MC's significant other, who is a singer in CR's corporate band, adore this tiny cockroach. CR is not that bad of a musician. MC on the other hand, is down right pathetic! MC really needs to take music lessons. Is anyone out there a musical instructor?

Let's talk about the agent that is a pussycat lover. PCL, short for pussycat lover, is a musician turned agent. Hum? Use your imagination to figure out the meaning of *this* nickname! PCL has a liking for flamboyant entertainers. I wonder why? Most of these acts are crass and the style of music is mindless. PCL represents an entertainer who incorporates sequenced music and vocal tracks. The show is all fake! The wanna-be aerobics teacher is way too busy performing kinetics. I get a full cardiovascular workout just watching the hip-jerking robot. Obviously, the entertainer needs oxygen to sing! I hear that PCL takes a heavy percentage for commission. I have no idea if PCL kicks back to the Entertainment Directors bags of cash for booking PCL's bands.

PCL also has a fancy for show dancers. You can catch PCL's significant other dancing in many shows around town. Hum? Do you think PCL likes quivering body movements on stage and behind closed bedroom doors? Why is it when cats lick their fur, they always throw up fur balls? Do you think it could be the combination of the fur and too much fish in their diet?

Let's talk about ethnicity of musicians. I am not a prejudiced person. God has blessed all his children with special talents. Unfortunately, some agents in town have a predilection for certain ethnic groups.

One agent in town strictly books bands that are of one ethnic race. Can we all just get along here? The agent is down right two-faced and miserable. Do not bother knocking on this agent's door if you are not of one sex and of one color. Good luck!

Most of these ethnic sterile groups have been dominating the music scene in Vegas for many decades. They are dinosaurs, and the reptilian creatures eat well. I would rather eat filet mignon for dinner than chopped liver. They are steadfastly grazing on cream-of-the-crop gigs.

An agent whom I will call GG, short for glitz and glamour, represents most of these acts. GG is extremely protective of the lounges in which they perform. You call those lounges "A" rooms. There are plenty of "B" and "C" rooms around town for entertainment acts. Usually, the more prestigious the casino, the better the budget is for entertainment.

GG has a horrendous habit of not returning phone calls. I wonder if GG's answering machine has a malfunction? I doubt it. Numerous bands are standing in line for GG. Be prepared. Bring plenty of water and camping gear. You might be standing in line for along, long, long time. GG is blatantly critical of entertainment acts that are not visually stimulating. Bands must wear fancy high-priced apparel. GG should be picky. After all, is it not true that Las Vegas is all about *glitz and glamour?*

Illustrations by Nick San Pedro © 2001

Las Vegas is a magnet for sleazy agents. They flock to Las Vegas and take advantage of the hungry musicians. The lower class agents mostly book "C" rooms. Musicians welcome any kind or work, no matter how little the gig pays. Musicians would even perform nude while standing on their heads to bring home the bones.

One slime agent in town is merciless towards musicians. The green ball of algae has the most degrading musical jobs in Vegas. The pond scum agent will send frantic music bands to all parts of Nevada that do not even exist on the map. The agent will skim twenty percent off the top of the microscopic budget. Very little bone fragments exist to pay the hungry musicians. Musicians will endure this financial abuse. They know other musicians are right around the corner to snag their job away from them.

Viper agents love to sink their venomous fangs into all willing participants in Vegas. One thing about snakes, they do not discriminate when they attack their victims. Musicians will deliberately throw themselves in the line of fire of venomous snake fangs just to get work.

A Green Mojave agent loves to slither it's scaly body on the streets of Vegas. The ill-looking agent looks as if a drug addict has narrowly escaped over-dosing and cheated death a thousand times. The emaciated agent will sink it's fangs into musicians' paychecks and suck twenty percent off the top of the casino lounge budget. Depending on the casino budget, the agent will take a bigger chunk of money for commission.

Musicians habitually infected with all the diseases agents spread though out the Las Vegas music scene, have no cure. No pills or shots exist for musicians to take to make their financial immune systems stronger. All musical agents in Vegas have the financial power over the weak musicians and are slithering all the way to the bank.

THREE

ENTERTAINMENT SCAMS

Do you ever wonder why you cannot wait to finish drinking your Rum and Coke and hightail it out of a lounge to go gamble? The casino executives want your money. The music acts in the lounges are corny for that reason only. The casinos in Las Vegas are not standing tall because of the revenue from liquor sales, but from the cash you drop gambling. I would rather gamble than be subjected to bombastic and vacuous entertainers. Dealers are even getting nauseous from the audio stench that these bands spew into the air. Does anyone have a pair of earplugs I can borrow? It is a well planned out scheme between the casino executives, Entertainment Directors and agents to play a psychological money game with your mind.

The land of entertainment is the land of "MAKE BELIEVE." Las Vegas is infested with entertainers that are making a mockery of famous artists. Why would you want to waste your money watching a fake performer when you can see the real thing? They say imitation is a form of flattery. It is a musical insult, in my opinion. It is just another money-making gimmick geared for all the suckers who buy tickets to these shows. The imposters even take advantage of the entertainment icons that are six feet under the ground. Elvis seems to be the favorite. Some of these copycats even go to the extreme of receiving cosmetic surgery to look like their idol. Most of the shows have sequenced music tracks. Is there anything in the world that is the real deal?

Las Vegas has a few extremely talented impersonators in the show rooms of major casinos. The shows will knock you off your saddle and take you for a hay ride. They have mastered their talent and I recommend spending your money on these well-produced shows. Famous artists are constantly performing in Vegas. Invest your money on the real thing. The dividends are worth it.

Las Vegas is home to an enormous money making entertainment scam. Music bands will lease a famous artist name or a famous band name to make money of your ignorance. The hyenas are making a killing. The agents booking these bands know they have a gold mine. You are not seeing or listening to the real deal. Usually, three or four bands with the same name perform at the same time, but in different casinos. Sounds a little perplexing, but you will get the hang of it. The music era of these bands is mostly from the 60's. No original band members exist in either bands. The bands' names resemble names of kitchen ware. Boy, I am getting hungry. Would anyone like to join me for a big plate of corn fritters?

FOUR

ENTERTAINMENT GUIDES

Las Vegas has an over-abundance of entertainment magazines for your entertainment enjoyment. When you check into your hotel room, more than likely, you will find one of these amusing magazines for your convenience. You can even find these magazines in grocery stores. What is up with that? It is just a matter of time before CR and MC book an organ grinder and monkey at the local grocery stores, since they have slot machines for your gambling pleasure.

Entertainment magazines have a list of all the shows currently being performed in Las Vegas and of future engagements. Usually, there is a list of lounge entertainment. Do not waste your time reading *this* section! Why would you want to listen to and watch the same old burnt-out assembly line haggard musicians? These brown bag bands even pass around the same generic song list. You can walk into a lounge casino any night of the week and hear the same songs at the same time. When you were a young kid going to school, did you get sick and tired of the same old peanut butter and jelly sandwiches your mother made for lunch?

Las Vegas is home to one of the most preposterous cable television entertainment shows you will *ever* see! The cheese-filled bag show airs every Saturday night before the midnight hour from a casino on the famous strip. The backdrop consists of antique cars. The show features two dumbfounded talk show hosts interviewing the most deranged and bizarre entertainment performers in Las Vegas. Obviously, the person who is in charge of finding these acts is suffering from a brain disorder called, "Cerebrosclerosis." I have heard that the entertainment acts receive no compensation for their appearance on the show. I can see why! The person with the brain disorder needs hospitalization and should not receive any compensation. The show is a complete failure because of the incompetency of the producers. Everyone involved in the show should drive away in one of the antique cars into the wild wild west.

FIVE

ENTERTAINERS SEEKING LAS VEGAS FOR EMPLOYMENT

Illustrations by Nick San Pedro © 2001

Las Vegas is in dire need of vibrant, expressive and refreshing musicians. It will be a cold day in hell before that metamorphosis occurs. Musicians think Vegas is a panacea for their musical woes. Think again! It will not happen in this city! If you are a musician and plan to make an Exodus to Vegas, make sure you say many prayers to God. Maybe, musical luck will be on your side when you arrive in Vegas. I have witnessed remarkably talented musicians that are perpetually out of work. Remember, it is all about *politics and money* in Vegas. It is a common epidemic in this city.

Only a few select entertainers will have an illustrious career in Vegas. The main object for an entertainer is to land an *indefinite contract* at a fancy, hotty-totty casino. It is virtually an unattainable dream. If you are a musician in the truest form, you will have a difficult time adjusting to the style of music that most bands are playing.

Here is some advice. You must have a prerequisite of Corn 101 to advance to Philosophy of Corn. Dress your self in a corn cob outfit and join a corny Top-40 band. More than likely, you might have to bite your tongue and swallow your musical creativity. Entertainment Directors can care less if you are a virtuoso in music. Well, it is about that time for me to watch an electrifying movie and eat a big bag of popcorn.

What is the definition of an *indefinite contract?* Does it mean what it sounds like? Does it mean that you will have financial security forever and ever? I remember reading about fairy tales ending in forever and ever. In this town, an *indefinite contract* is a duration of time the casino has hired an entertainment act to perform. The time span can range from a few months to a few years or longer. The upper echelon casinos specifically reserve their show rooms for indefinite extravaganzas.

It is a completely different animal when it pertains to a casino *lounge contract*. A majority of lounges have a steady rotation of bands. Usually, it is a one to two week run. A handful of Top-40 bands will have longer runs at certain strip casino lounges. Las Vegas has more musicians than gigs. Keeping that in mind, musicians resemble rapacious sharks in a feeding frenzy when an agent throws them gig bait. All of a sudden, I feel like canceling my vacation plans to go to the beach.

SIX

ENTERTAINMENT DIRECTORS

Illustrations by Nick San Pedro © 2001

Most Entertainment Directors are in a cloud of musical bewilderment. They are jumping on and off the musical band wagon from one week to another. With a whimsical change of heart, like fickle teenagers, they might sever entertainers *indefinite contracts* for the flavor of the week style of music. When a style of ethnic music is en vogue, every casino is in competition to attract potential ethnic clientele.

One style of music keeps dangling like a scarf out of the band wagon's back seat window. Please, can anyone roll up the window? Almost every casino in town reserves nights for this particular music theme. CR has a bevy of bands that perform this style of music and they are everywhere. As I told you before, CR monopolizes a huge portion of the entertainment acts in Vegas. *Yuck!*

Vegas must offer more exciting ways to "trip the light fantastic"? It is not such a bad idea to go to the local grocery store and see if the organ grinder and monkey are performing. I can even play the one arm bandit and eat a bag of corn nuts. I really think I have too much corn in my diet. Too much of one thing can be bad for one's health.

One common denominator that ninety-five percent of Entertainment Directors share is, "THEY ARE RUDE AS HELL!" Who died and made them the "SUPERIOR BEING?" Most Entertainment Directors' delusions of grandeur surpass the height of the tallest casinos in Vegas.

Do you ever remember watching the cartoon *Rocky and Bullwinkle?* Well, they are graduates from *Bullwinkle's Corner* and *Mr. Know It All.* A majority of Entertainment Directors will never accept phone calls. If you leave a message with their secretaries, either male or female, the Entertainment Director conveniently never receives the message. If you have the honor of speaking to the *Know It Alls,* their music schedule is conveniently made out for the year. They just do not have time to speak to the common folk. Unfortunately, CR and MC already promised them a briefcase of loot in favor of booking their cornmeal bands. Hum? I need to attend *Bullwinkle's Corner* to become a *Know It All.*

Mammoth corporations own and operate the majority of casinos in Vegas. The word "boundaries" does not exist in the dictionary when it comes to one "greedy hands" corporation. The corporation horticulturists are spreading Miracle-Gro though out the entire valley and their properties are sprouting up like tomato vines.

The Lamborghini of all Entertainment Directors reigns over these well-nourished plush lands. This is one top notch Entertainment Director that comes with a few inexplicable discrepancies. I would think someone with a prominent title would want to the have the appearance of nobility. The Entertainment Director looks as if a Cabbage Patch Doll with stringy blonde hair and glasses had a bad day in *Mr. Rogers Neighborhood*!

I must say that I have enormous amount of admiration for this work horse. BW, short for bigwig, climbed the corporate tree and succeeded in making a cozy bed in the top branches. Quickly how one forgets one's roots and a superfluous ego takes command of one's self. Mechanics tell me to keep my tires properly inflated for better road performance.

BW's faithfulness to the longevity of *indefinite contracts* is remarkable. Stunned and amazed, I cannot comprehend BW's choice of musical bands that have the honor of signing these precious jewels. BW signed PCL's flamboyant aerobics instructor to an *indefinite contact*. What a travesty! Sadly, BW will book a hefty portion of CR's atrocious bands. Hum? I detect the aroma of kickback money! At times, BW will experience capricious mood swings and slice spectacular music acts *indefinite contracts* into iddy-biddy pieces. I often ask myself, "How did those mundane, repugnant and mechanical looking entertainers dodge the bullet line?" Hum? I do not know the answer. Oh, I get it! CR must have put money in the gun.

BW has a pseudo-agent that is in charge of hiring entertainment for the ethnic theme night at one of BW's casinos. Where did BW find this archaic snapping turtle? The wanna-be Entertainment Director has the finesse of a termite! AST, short for archaic snapping turtle, will sometimes hire out-of-town ethnic bands. AST suffocating personality interferes with anyone who wants to talk business. The *Know It All* will go behind BW's back and pay entertainment acts money out of AST's back pocket.

The budget that BW allocates for these events is minimal. AST only gets a certain percentage from the cover charge at the door. The out-of-town entertainment acts are under false pretenses about the entertainment budget for this particular event. AST also throws in transportation. If an act from out-of-town wants to perform at any casino in town, they expect the same budget and accommodations. Most other casinos will not throw in any perks for out-of-town acts. AST then demands out-of-town acts to sign with AST exclusively. Eventually, BW will have to cough up the extra income for these out-of-town acts. AST cannot be making that much of a profit from the cover charge. Hum? I think AST should go back to school and brush up on proper business skills!

Let me talk about several other Entertainment Directors who reside on "Entertainment Directors Lane." Maybe, tourists can buy sight-seeing maps to this neighborhood. Hum? No! No! No! That is a horrible idea! All of us are better off buying maps to famous stars' homes in another state.

Now I feel a special camaraderie with all of you, let's start calling these pompous corn connoisseurs E.D.s.

One E.D. whom I will call LL, short for lurking lurch, is creepier than a graveyard. This poltergeist will hold musical seances with CR and MC and the spirits end up playing at LL's lounge. More than likely, CR and MC will kick back LL a coffin full of cash.

One ghostly act always has returned dates. This is one of MC's concoction of sequenced bands. This is one bad batch of witch's brew that cannot even play their instruments. LL can give a flying broomstick if bands have talent. Their choreography is as flaccid as an overripe banana. I believe LL has a sick perverted mind. The elevated stage at LL's lounge makes viewing of entertainers crotch area a titillating experience. Hum? Now I know why LL prefers female entertainers. You can always find LL lurking at the end of the music stage in a murky daze eating a corn dog. Hum? I wonder if LL's best friends are ghosts and goblins? *Oooooooohhhhhh!!!!!!! Aaaaaahhhhhhhhhh!!!!!!*

25

Shall we continue strolling down "Entertainment Directors Lane?" Yes! The fun has just begun. I have an uncontrollable urge to knock on the door of TW, short for the weasel. Weasels have a propensity for being sly and sneaky. TW even has beady eyes and the nose of this carnivore species. TW is the E.D. of two casinos owned by the same corporation.

The cunning weasel also moonlights as a musician. Most of the bands that TW hires will have to accommodate the meat eater's demand to play in the band. Do you think TW's superiors have noticed this sly maneuver? I doubt it. Casino executives can care less about the entertainment. TW has free rein to roam the grounds to prey on chickens. The chickens are musicians. One would think that chickens would get a little nervous in spotting a weasel. As I said a million times before, musicians need to work. Musicians will endure any work environment to bring home the butter for the cornbread. TW should stop picking on chickens and find some other kind of food to eat. Hum? I think TW should start eating Corn Flakes!

Illustrations by Nick San Pedro © 2001

Has it not been a fun-packed trip so far? I personally like stopping to see the scenic views. I really like looking in E.D.s back yards to see if they have any dirty laundry lying around.

Let us look in the backyard of SR, short for self-righteous. This *Know It All* graduated with honors from *Bullwinkle's Corner*. SR dominates the music lounge at a mega casino on the strip. Rumor has it, that SR and CR are close confidants. Every now and then, you can catch these two squirrels sucking down Brandy at SR's lounge. I think they should be drinking corn whiskey. Need I say more? Yes! SR's lounge is an "A" room. Most of CR's regurgitating bands have the privilege of performing at this pearl-in-the-oyster lounge. SR is somewhat self-complacent and hesitates to hire different bands. Hum? I wonder why? CR must give this chipmunk a steady supply of acorns. You know, MONEY!!!!!!!!!!!!

Can E.D.s also moonlight as magicians? Obviously, some magicians must need two jobs to make ends meet. I have the utmost respect for magicians. They have mastered their skill in wizardry, the sleight of hand deception and mind deception. Hey, I can only handle so much mind deception. E.D.s have mastered their mind games and to have one that is a magician is frightening!

MM, short for master of manipulation, is the E.D. of a casino in the outskirts of town. The room is a "C" room. Out of nowhere, MM turns it into a prodigious "A" room. Is that what you would call an illusion? Only in MM's make believe mind! The lounge is awful! The budget for entertainment is infinitesimal. MM scrutinizes promotional material as if the bands were to perform for The Queen of England. I have been a spectator at one of MM's magic shows and the room was naked as a *Penthouse* Center Fold! I will commend MM for the brilliant magic show. I appreciate all forms of artistic creativity. MM should appreciate all forms of musical creativity and shouldn't fret over whether or not the lounge is full of spectators. Speaking of all this abracadabra, can anyone perform magic on my lack of finances? The IRS has the best disappearing act in the country.

E.D.s come from all walks of life. I mean that figuratively! One E.D. in town was once a trapeze artist for a clown-filled casino. The casino is still standing and is still clown-filled. FCA, short for former circus act, works for the same corporation and is the E.D. of two of their casino properties. I think I know what all of you are thinking. Does FCA only hire circus acts for the entertainment at FCA's casino lounges? Well, guess what? FCA books CR's same old juggling acts in the lounges. CR will kick back money to FCA to buy clown outfits. I neglected to inform all of you, that most of the E.D.s in Vegas do all of their banking at CR's private bank.

I find that cockroaches are fascinating little creatures. It appears that Las Vegas is having one hell of a time getting rid of just one. The expiration date on my can of Raid is today. Hum? I know. The city of Las Vegas should call the Orkin Man!

Variety should be the spice of life. My taste buds love to experience titillating and tingling sensations. A well-rounded diet promotes a healthy life style.

An E.D. whom I will call ST, short for school teacher, only serves corn tortillas in the lounge ST represents. Obviously, ST has a distaste for flour tortillas. The same corn chowder bands have permeated ST's lounges for many years. ST's appearance is that of a school teacher with prim and proper mannerisms. I believe ST was a professor at *Bullwinkle's Corner*. ST discriminates against bands that are of one sex. Come on! We are living in the new millennium for corn sake! ST is a heavy advocate of *indefinite contracts* and that business characteristic warrants a standing ovation.

ST has an ancient performer who is on display almost daily. I would rather visit the La Brea Tar Pits and learn about different types of fossils. The entertainer is the epitome of run-over street trash. Rumor has it, that the entertainer had a few visits from the law in the past. Supposedly, the entertainer's sleaze bag hand was in the drug jar too many times. I do not judge one's past behavior. People have the choice to change their life and turn over a new leaf. Obviously, the musical leaf crumbled many years ago for this time-warp specimen! The aged specimen has remained the same through out the years. I wonder if ST's favorite subject in school was Ancient History?

A petrified band that performs at ST's lounge has had an *indefinite contract* for four or five years. More than likely, ST will sign the band for five more years. The theme of the music has something to do with water and sand. I would rather visit the beaches in Southern California and listen to The Beach Boys music. I believe MC formed this band along, long, long time ago in the great white country.

ST has a sensational entertainer performing in the show room of the casino. Hum? I think I will treat my taste buds to a refreshing Pina Colada while watching the extravaganza in the show room.

One scraggily old E.D. in town will hire entertainment acts geared for the older generation. The acts have been a staple in the Las Vegas music scene for many years. The entertainers somewhat still possess the energy and pizzazz to capture a crowd. This Entertainment Director's business savvy just gripes my ass. A close friend of mine revealed to me the budget that the entertainers receive for their performance. BT, short for budget thief, will take two hundred dollars off the top of the budget. Usually, the bands perform for three nights. Hum? Does that add up to six hundred dollars? The bottom dweller is not only ripping off the musicians, but the casino executives. Can you imagine the financial chaos when CR and MC have their glutinous hands in the budget pie? I would love to be a fly on the wall listening to these budget heists. Can you believe that MC booked the bad batch of witch's brew at this lounge? What *was* this corn pop thinking? The place probably was in a complete stage of pandemonium and the audience ran for their lives!

A high profile family own and operates several casinos that cater to the locals. It is one big happy 24/7 family picnic. Business is booming. Bill Gates might have a run for the money with *this* yacht sailing family!

AK, short for ass kisser, is the E.D. of three family casinos. Unfortunately, Cockroach Productions supplies most of the corn chip entertainment for AK's lounges. The casino executives vehemently deny any out-of-state lounge entertainment. The budget allocated for lounge entertainment has taken a nose dive. The casino executives concentrate all their undivided attention to the gamblers. The bigwigs treat gamblers to thousands of dollars in food and hotel room comps every day of the week. It would cost too much money to accommodate out-of-state entertainment with room and board. That is far from the truth! Casino executives want the money in their pockets.

31

A close musician friend of mine performed at one of the family casinos. My friend packed the lounge and the casino executives fired my friend. Unfortunately, exceptional musicians have a dead end career in this city.

The family named one of their casinos after a town famous for its food and style of music. One would think they have a lounge specifically catering to this style of music. You must to be kidding! The absent minded casino executives must have had their faces in a pot of Crayfish and forgot the style of music. One of the lounge's style of music has something to do with the color Kelly. I appreciate all styles of ethnic music, but this was an inappropriate musical decision. All E.D.s must obey orders from the casino executives. If not, they will lose their jobs.

Let's talk about nepotism with this diamond drenched family. Someone in the family married a musician. The musician's band is a family band. The family siblings look like tired goats trying to climb a mountain. Well, guess what? The tired goats climbed to the top of the mountain and found flourishing green lands. They are on a rotation schedule with all the properties. The band's appearance is detestable. Their style of music sounds as if goats triggered an echo-filled avalanche. Hum? I wonder if there is anyone in the yacht sailing family I can marry?

The politics in this family casino empire includes the All Mighty Lord. Religion of all denominations should aid people in believing in faith and to restore structure in their lives. Why is it, that certain people who say they follow in the Lord's footsteps will abuse and twist religion to their own financial gain? Supposedly, someone who preaches the Lord's divine words is a friend of the family dynasty. A musician who attends this reverend's church is conveniently performing at the family casinos. Hum? It should be the House of the Lord not the House of the Casino!

Favoritism even spills over into the gaming department. The significant other of a close friend of the family is a floor supervisor that once had a lower position at one of the casinos. Well, guess what? Out of nowhere, the floor supervisor has a higher title and all the perks that come with this promotion. I wish I had a pillow job with silk pillow cases. Maybe I could sleep better!

For your viewing pleasure, the family casinos hire the best eye candy cocktail waitresses in Las Vegas! Most all the Twin Peaks moved to Las Vegas from Silicon Valley! Cocktails! Cocktails! Cocktails!

I neglected to tell all of you folks that CR moonlighted as an Entertainment Director for two casinos. A well-known casino mogul bought one of the casinos that CR dominated. The mogul fired the entire casino personnel and shut down the casino. Can you imagine a tiny cockroach with a hobo stick searching for a new dwelling?

Remember the E.D. I called BT? CR filled the E.D. seat at BT's casino. A big corporation bought the casino while CR was sitting on the throne. Soon after the purchase of the casino, CR had to step down from the throne and hand it over to BT. Oh what a pity! I wish the Mayor of Las Vegas would pass a law banning this pestering insect from stealing money from the casinos and musicians.

The State of Nevada has casinos in every nook and cranny. Nevada's nickname is the Silver State. A more appropriate nick name is, "CR and MC's Sucker State."

CR and MC's cockroach empire extends to all areas apart from Las Vegas. They will send some of their flesh eating bacteria entertainment acts to Reno, Laughlin, Primm, Mesquite, Jackpot, and where ever there is a casino. CR will send acts to New Jersey, Chicago, California, Arizona and on cruise ships. Hum? The next time you decide to go on a cruise, Cockroach Productions probably has supplied the entertainment. *Yuck!* I would rather read a book and fall asleep to the sounds of the ocean!

Most of the E.D.s of the out-of-town casinos are under the same CR and MC hypnotic money trance as their counterparts in Vegas. It is an infectious disease quickly spread by one cockroach.

One of the state line casinos has an E.D. with this contagious disease. The confused lunatic must experience mental hallucinations. If you have the honor of talking to the nut case, you will be in a mental stupor of your own. If you send promotional material to the E.D. for possible bookings, it mysteriously disappears. If the style of music you have submitted to the E.D. is what was requested, the music venue has mysteriously changed to another style. *Wow!* Does *this* scenario sound familiar? Unfortunately, CR and MC made it to the finish line before anyone else. The Entertainment Director obviously has a liking for the bad batch of witch's brew and their horrifying performance with splintered broomsticks. *Ouch!* The Entertainment

Director has the wart-faced and hook-nosed creatures performing on selected Friday and Saturday nights.

Occasionally, Entertainment Directors of out-of-town casinos will hire entertainment acts that are from other musical agencies. Hum? CR and MC must have been napping in the Cockroach Hotel and lost out on eating some crumbs! The agent that only hires musicians from one ethnic group has a grip on a couple of casinos in town, as well as out-of-town. Laughlin has plenty of casinos that supply lounge entertainment.

A casino in Laughlin has an E.D. who is persnickety as a cat in heat. I think the E.D. and the agent both share the same affection for musicians of one ethnic group. I believe PWOS, short for pretentious worn-out swine, has had a few of CR's Leprosarium bands performing at Persnickety's Lounge in the past. I have heard that the quality of the budget at Persnickety's Lounge is now that of a denuded rain forest. Musicians can care less about the budget. As I mentioned a billion times before, musicians will sell their soul to the devil to bring home the food on the bottom of the pitch fork. If you try calling the E.D. of Persnickety's Lounge, your call is as transparent as *Casper the Ghost*. The E.D. will never return your call. More than likely, PWOS has sealed the entertainment acts in a zip locked food bag. It is just a matter of time before a cockroach will invade the security of a zip locked food bag.

Most Entertainment Directors have a lazy and easy job. You can always find a La-Z-Boy in *their* velvet and leather coated office! They implicitly refuse to hire musical entertainment without first viewing a video of the entertainment act. If an established musical band has been performing in Vegas for decades, they still demand a video. They are even too lazy to venture out of their crushed velvet office to view an entertainment act that is performing in the casino lounge next door to their casino. They reserve their precious energy only to cash their platinum paycheck and take kickback money from CR.

Every casino that has music entertainment employs Entertainment Directors. I can talk about these corn huskers until I am yellow in the face. I should change it to green in the face like the pea soup scene from the movie, *The Exorcist*! It is the same story, but different Entertainment Directors. It is all about *politics and money* and CR occupies most of the seats of the musical government in Las Vegas. The constituencies that CR governs are musicians, E.D.s and other agents. If you have a recusant personality, you will not survive under CR's reign. CR calls all the shots and all people involved had better obey orders if they want their financial rewards. In a way, CR is the Godfather of CR's own musical Mafia. If the Mafia existed today in Vegas, as it was in the old days, CR would not exist.

SEVEN

AGENTS DRESS CODES FOR ENTERTAINERS

CR has stringent guidelines for the appearance of musicians. CR prefers to dress one sex like tawdry pornographic models and the other sex to dress like clowns. Can you imagine pornographic magazines with clowns and tawdry models? That is a wee bit on the dark side for me. Hum? Maybe, you can catch this act at one of the many gentleman's clubs in Vegas. I have visited most of these clubs and I have not seen any clowns as of yet!

One of CR's fertilizer bands has two siblings playing instruments that look like hokey farm hands. These two look-a-likes must have bought their stage clothes at the cheapest thrift store in Vegas. I wonder if they bought two items for the price of one? Do you think they might have picked corn in the corn fields of Iowa? You can watch the performance of the double suited look-a-likes at two of the diamond drenched family casinos. Hum? I guess when you watch their performance, you have double the fun.

MC's significant other looks like a petite Christmas tree with way too much tinsel. I do not know about you holiday enthusiasts, but I like my Christmas tree evenly decorated so it will not tip over onto all the Christmas gifts. MC's bad batch of witch's brew has the appearance of corn muffins made with corn starch. *Yuck!* That would taste horrible! I already informed all of you where these oddities perform.

One of CR's bands is a throw back to the early 80's. The three singers that front the band wear the same outdated sleazy spandex costumes. The three singers have no musical talent what-so-ever! The singers are of the same height and ethnic background. I have heard of double vision, but not triple vision! My eyes experience fatigue watching the made up stiff puppet dolls perform CR's decomposed choreography. Las Vegas lounge entertainers should desperately seek Paula Abdul. The dead puppets have recurring stage shows at the yacht sailing family casinos.

Illustrations by Nick San Pedro © 2001

One of CR's bands has a front person that looks as if a flame has been burning out of control for years. Make sure you bring a fire extinguisher to this char-broiled fiasco! The condiments on each side of the flame look as if wilted lettuce and mayonnaise soaked hamburger buns were baking in the afternoon sun. A musician in the band has the appearance of a sickly anorexic patient recently released from the hospital. Hum? Do you think the sickly musician should eat a few burnt hamburgers with the condiments?

Bon Appétit! Every now and then you can catch the ant-filled picnic performing at LL's lounge.

A common entertainment saying in Vegas is, "People hear with their eyes while watching entertainers perform." A Las Vegas entertainer's appearance should be high class with glittery apparel and be physically appealing to the audience. Not all Las Vegas entertainers come with the package deal of physical beauty and talent. If they did, I think Hollywood would have noticed them by now.

Remember the diamond drenched family that owns several casinos in Vegas? A generic music band has a rotating schedule with two of the casinos. I do not know if CR represents this act. I have heard that the leader of the band is inter-linked with the family. I have deep concern for one of the musician's health. Unfortunately, the musician's physique is larger than the average performer in Vegas. I have visions of the unhealthy musician experiencing a heart attack in the middle of a performance. Hum? This on stage scenario would have all the drama and theatrics of a Hollywood movie! Lights! Action! Camera!

Remember the bands that will lease a famous artist name to make money off of your ignorance? CR represents one of these artificial pitiful bands. While watching the three piteous front singers perform, a sense of empathy will completely dominate your inner soul. Their stage show is the epitome of corn. The choreography looks as if three anthropoids are stuck in quicksand and desperately seeking a rescue from sinking to the bottom of the earth. The Coast Guard would have to call off their search for the sand covered mammals. More than likely, the musicians in the band bought their wardrobe at a clown garage sale. I would think with CR's wealth that CR could afford appropriate apparel for these multi-colored abstract paintings on the wall. You can catch the anthropoids carrying multi-colored abstract paintings on to a few lounge casinos around town, including BT's lounge.

I mentioned earlier that MC hires musicians with missing teeth. I adamantly advocate oral hygiene. When you meet someone for the first time, you automatically focus on the person's smile. A beautiful smile with perfect teeth is a sign that the people care about their physical appearance. Obviously, MC could care less about the oral hygiene of musicians. MC's consumed with the bands sounding and looking like corn stalks in a corn field in Iowa.

Illustrations by Nick San Pedro © 2001

MC has a band performing at an up scale casino on the strip. You would think that the E.D. of this casino would want classy congenial entertainers performing at the lounge. MC probably told the toothless corn stalk not to talk to the E.D. and to hide the rotten corn kernels in the musician's mouth. The band should have a tip jar in front of the stage stating, "PLEASE HELP US! WE NEED MONEY FOR DENTURES!" Rumor has it that the front person of the band, who by the way has a full set of teeth, departed from the band to sing back-up vocals for a famous recording artist and movie star. I heard through the musical grapevine that MC had a temper tantrum over the singer for neglecting to give a two week notice. Now, if you had an opportunity to perform with a sensuous, gorgeous and delicious looking super star, I seriously doubt that you would fret over MC's childlike behavior. If I was the singer, I would have jammed a baby pacifier down MC's throat so MC could never talk again.

Another one of CR's bands has a front person that is notably provocative. Is there a fine line drawn between sensual eloquence and carnal knowledge? Obviously, the entertainer has a latent tendency for a career in rated XXX movies! The upper frontal thorax of the entertainer is overwhelmingly exposed as if two pieces of bread were craving a slice of lunch meat. Hum? A sandwich made with plastic bread sounds unappetizing. I do not know if all of you have Epicurean curiosities, but I never could acquire a taste for imitation food products. More than likely, CR prefers toasted bagels with imitation cream cheese. You can catch the open-faced sandwich performing bi-monthly at SR's pearl-in-the-oyster lounge.

The music industry has unleashed a surging explosion of same sex bands. CR's frantic attempt to reproduce this sensation has gone awry. The number one ingredient for a successful same sex band is youth. The second ingredient is a good looking face that will captivate the opposite sex. The third ingredient that completes the recipe, is a singing voice that harmonizes well with the other vocals in the band. CR has not one ingredient correct in *this* recipe! CR's impulsive decision in the choice of ingredients for this distasteful recipe looks as if unemployed aging magazine models are desperately seeking a career change as wanna-be pop vocalists. I would rather watch MTV and look at the real deal! Occasionally, you can watch the faded magazine faces perform at SR's lounge.

When I watch a performer sing, I want to feel the emotion of the song and watch the articulation in the singer's face. If the singer executes the meaning of the song in a fluid manner, then the singer has done a good job in captivating an audience.

One of CR's lounge lizard bands has a front person that looks as if they sucked on a lemon and are grimacing to find the next musical note. The wanna-be pop sensation struggles with limited vocal range. I feel that I have just bitten in to a bitter lemon seed watching the singer perform! I have heard that the singer is critical with other musicians in the band. CR and the lemon sucker should set up a lemonade stand on the corner of Tropicana and Las Vegas Boulevard! Do you think they would have any customers? I seriously doubt it. The lemonade would be too bitter to drink!

CR's stable of entertainment acts embodies a menagerie of preposterous characters. One of CR's bands is reminiscent of a young child and a dog in a tornado that end up intertwined in a land of make believe. The front person of this band is exceptionally talented and delivers a riveting performance. The entertainer wears a yellow wig that looks as if scarecrows plucked out the hair and made a crow's nest. Hum? I wonder if the corn fields of Iowa could employ a yellow haired scarecrow that sings a song about a yellow road? You can catch the scarecrow and the corn field friends performing at BW's lounge every Friday and Saturday night.

Every now and then, I like to engage in outdoor activities. CR's favorite all time outdoor sport is watching the many animal species roam the desert of Las Vegas. Obviously, CR's pet band has an array of wild life only CR can appreciate. The front person of this zoo-filled animal cage has the appearance of an anorexic giraffe wearing a coal black short hair wig. Can you imagine viewing an anorexic giraffe's genital area at LL's lounge? I believe Las

Vegas is offering a new form of entertainment featuring animated cartoon characters. More than likely, CR climbs the legs of the giraffe for a panoramic view of the Las Vegas desert. You can watch the toothpick giraffe and the zoo-filled friends performing at LL's lounge on a regular basis.

As we continue with our lesson in Zoology, CR has a zoo cage reserved for whacked-out impersonators. The gallery of impersonators runs the entertainment gamut. The city of Las Vegas is a Mecca for exploiting the names of famous entertainers. Can you believe that Las Vegas has a cross-dressing Elvis? I have no idea if CR or MC came up with this gimmick. More than likely, they did! The ambi-sexual looking character performs at a restaurant, not at a casino lounge. Can you imagine walking through a casino with your children and finding this whacked-out monstrosity performing? Your children could take this thing to their school's "Show and Tell Day".

I have seen a handful of CR's counterfeit acts. I am tenaciously against entertainers making money by using and abusing the name of a famous artist. The performers' half-ass attempt to replicate a famous stage persona is dismal at best. The list of famous people includes Madonna, Marilyn Monroe, Rod Stewart, Frank Sinatra, Sammy Davis Jr., Elvis, Neil Diamond and many more.

Illustrations by Nick San Pedro © 2001

One of CR's impersonators portrays Madonna and Marilyn Monroe. The over-processed bleach blonde's attempt to sound and look like the two bombshells have backfired. The deceiver looks as if a bomb exploded and the flying shrapnel shredded the impostor's vocal cords and destroyed the charlatan's charred bleach blonde hair. The dingbat performs with MC and the bad batch of witch's brew. Hum? I wonder if LL and the charlatan take midnight rides on a flying splintered broomstick? *Ouch*! That has to hurt!

Frank Sinatra and Elvis impersonators are a penny a dozen in Vegas. If you have seen one, you have seen them all. The Elvis impersonators come in all shapes and sizes. I have witnessed a surge in overweight Elvis impostors. BW and MM fancy the overweight Elvis look-a-likes. The thinner Elvis impostors perform in the show rooms of certain strip casinos. I have seen a few Frank Sinatra impostors and they need to wear blue contact lenses to look more authentic. The Frank Sinatra impostors should have a Ava Gardner look-a-like hanging off their arm. Now, that is authenticity!

Remember the entertainer that attends the church of the reverend who is friends with the diamond drenched family? The entertainer moonlights as a Neil Diamond impostor. The fake entertainer lacks the appearance and finesse of Neil Diamond's stage persona. While watching the limp performer, it looks as if young kids made a big blob of nothing out of Play-Dough and are pretending that the big blob of nothing can sing. Hum? I think I would rather watch young kids play with Ken and Barbie.

MC will import impersonators from the great white country. Many famous entertainers come from this wonderful country and should not reflect on the non-quality of entertainers MC employs. In the future, Las Vegas will soon be the home to one of the white country's most famous singing entertainer.

Most of MC's fraudulent performers will perform at BT's lounge. I personally have not been a witness to any performances of these impostors. MC has no conception of entertainers with exceptional talent. All of MC's entertainment acts lack talent. I think MC employs inadequate performers because MC is an inept musician. If you are out and about in Las Vegas and want a barrel full of laughs, you must watch one of MC's musical acts. The acts are the best comedy shows you will *ever* see! Hum? BW should hire MC's musical acts to perform at BW's new comedy club. BW could book it as, "MC's Corn Comedy Hour." *Ha! Ha! Ha!*

BW has a fancy for hiring hard rock tribute bands. I do not know if CR supplies BW with this type of fraud entertainment. Unfortunately, this type of tribute bands offends the older generation. The new comedy club at one of BW's casinos, was once the home to hard rock tribute bands. The casino executives placed the table games right in front of the lounge. The loud and obtrusive music made it difficult for the players to enjoy themselves gambling. Most of the high rollers packed up their chips and went elsewhere to gamble. I can see why! Most of the band's music sounded as if construction workers were imploding a casino on the strip! Noise! Noise! Noise! Most of the tribute band's stage appearance looks as if they bought stage clothing at a yard sale for twenty-five cents.

BW should consider who is the typical Las Vegas gambler. It certainly is not teenagers! Can you believe BW loaded up a moving truck with the tribute bands and moved them into another casino that caters to the older generation? Hum? I wonder if BW has a latent sexual tendency for wanna-be rock stars? Is anyone hungry for a tender piece of meat?

A handful of impersonators around town is not under CR's hypnotic roach trance. An acquaintance of mine produces a show jammed-packed with the authenticity of the famous artists portrayed. As I mentioned before, I dislike imitations and this is the only show of impersonators that accomplish their stage persona. You can close your eyes and have the overwhelming sensation that the famous artist is singing just to you.

The producer of this show is also a musician. The musician has had an eleven year *indefinite contract* at one of the strip casinos. More than likely, the musician will have this chocolate covered strawberry gig as long as the lights keep twinkling in Vegas. I recommend stopping by this early morning party at the end of the strip! The band is amazing! One of the lead singers has a voice that Ann Wilson would appreciate.

The casino at the end of strip is home to some of the finest female impersonators in Vegas. If you want to see a spectacular show, you need to watch the fellows portraying their favorite female artist. It is androgyny at it's best.

I bet all of you are wondering what MC and CR's exterior looks like. All of us already know what their interior resembles. PURGATORY! MC always wears a corn cob outfit with a cell phone as a fashion accessory. CR really does look like a cockroach wearing two-toned fancy shoes.

Do you ever remember watching the cartoon *Gumby and Pokey*? CR is *Gumby* and MC is *Pokey*. They are mechanical little clay people. Would all of you like to hear an everyday conversation between these two stick figures?

"Hey *Pokey!*"

"Yes, *Gumby?*"

"What kind of adventure shall we have today, *Pokey?*"

"We can have the same adventure we have every day, *Gumby.*"

"Okay, *Pokey.*"

"Let me jump on your back and we can ride to all the casinos in Vegas, *Pokey.*"

"Okay, *Gumby.*"

"We can put all of our corn bands in the lounges and rob all the money from the musicians, *Pokey.*"

"Okay, *Gumby.*"

"All we have to do is kick back the Entertainment Directors bags of money, *Pokey.*"

"Okay, Gumby."

"*Weeeeeeeee*, this is so much fun, *Pokey.*"

"Yes, *Gumby.*"

As we all know in the cartoon, *Gumby* and *Pokey* were good Samaritans. They would never inflict evil or harm anyone. CR and MC should watch the cartoon to learn a few pointers in honesty.

EIGHT

ONE AGENT'S CONTROL OF LAS VEGAS ENTERTAINMENT

Illustrations by Nick San Pedro © 2001

CR's cockroach hotel has full capacity year round. CR has a heavy hold on the majority of the acts CR represents. If a band decides to use CR, CR will hound the band to sign an *exclusive contract* for a specific duration of time. Signing on the dotted line could be the beginning of the end for many of the bands. CR enthusiastically hustles to find work for the bands for about the first six months. After that, the bands are in a downward mud slide to oblivion. CR has a small colony of bands that get the imperial treatment and manage to escape CR's musical guillotine.

Las Vegas is saturated with bands that experiences work deprivation and CR takes advantage of this situation. Bands that sign an *exclusive contract* with CR soon find out that they forget to read between the fine lines. If bands book themselves in a casino that CR previously had them perform, CR demands the commission. Well, that is typical cockroach behavior. Cockroaches will always find crumbs to eat.

On occasion, CR will conduct business with other musical agents. Unfortunately, most agents will succumb to CR's business trickery.

I mentioned earlier, that a few casinos on the strip fired CR and they refuse to hire CR's entertainment. CR will desperately sway the agents who are in charge of hiring the lounge entertainment, to have CR's bands perform at their lounges. CR will kick back a diminutive amount of money to the agents, since all parties involved have to split the commission.

Illustrations by Nick San Pedro © 2001

Remember the agent I called GG? GG is the entertainment chief in charge at one of the lounges that CR can no longer penetrate. I guess the casino executives called the Orkin Man. GG is probably one of the most honest agents in town. Since GG acquired CR's previous lounge, I have not seen any of CR's colony of cockroach bands performing at GG's lounge. You can never under-estimate the tenacity of a cockroach. Only time will tell if GG adopts a new family pet.

The agent PCL has a colossal amount of disdain for CR's vicious business demeanor. CR and MC committed a dirty deed behind PCL's back. The dirty deed plot has a cast of characters I have already introduced to all of you. The front singer, who performs with the delicious recording artist and movie star, plays the lead role. The lemon sucker has the co-lead role. The best supporting roles belong to the music band that MC has performing at a casino lounge on the strip. The extra roles belong to the lemon sucker's music band. PCL is the casting agent. CR and MC are the directors.

Here is the dirty plot. PCL originally arranged with the E.D. of the casino where MC's band is now performing, to have the lemon sucker's band audition for an *indefinite contract*. The back-up singer for the delicious movie star was the front singer of the lemon sucker's band. The Entertainment Director disliked the lemon sucker and the musicians in the band, except for the singer. CR and MC smelled the opportunistic odor in the air and commandeered the singer. CR had one of MC's toothless corn stalk bands replace the original band. PCL and the lead singer are bitter enemies to this day. PCL and the lemon sucker still conduct music business. CR and PCL have hissing and scratching cat fights daily. CR and the lemon sucker have been friends for decades. CR has the lemon sucker playing at a casino on the corner of Tropicana and Las Vegas Blvd.

Illustrations by Nick San Pedro © 2001

NINE

LEADER OF THE BAND

Illustrations by Nick San Pedro © 2001

A breed of musician exists in Las Vegas that is the most egotistical and selfish animal you will *ever* meet! It is the

"LEADER OFTHE BAND!" Who died and made them "KING TUT" or "QUEEN NEFERTITI?" The narcissistic mirror lovers believe God's creation of them exists just for the peasants to adore and bestow unremitting affection. Most of these image conscious and spot light peacocks have minimal talent at best! They forget that their music band is the foundation they are standing on, not the stage. In some cases, the foundation is the sequenced music tracks. They hoard their treasures and pay the peasants one loaf of bread for a night's work.

The average pay for a casino lounge musician is one hundred dollars per night. Typical casino lounge entertainment is five to six nights a week. The math adds up to five or six hundred dollars per week. Most of you probably think that is not bad pay for a week's work. It is pennies when it comes to the outlandish paycheck the flaunting peacocks take home per week.

Remember the three anthropoids sinking in quicksand? Rumor has it, that the three deplucked peacocks demand one thousand dollars each per week. After CR's commission and the sickly three peacocks three thousand dollars, very little bird seeds are on the bottom of the bird cage to disseminate among the peasant musicians. The featherless peacocks treat their musicians as if they were prisoners chained to a dark and damp dungeon wall with rats scouring on the ground.

Not all front people are the leader of the band. Some musicians simply cannot sing. Most of them have inadequate communication skills and cannot talk to an audience. They lack the physical characteristics to be a front person. As I mentioned before, it is all about *glitz and glamour* in Vegas.

One of these non-singing peacock musicians has been performing with the colorless peacocks for decades. The musician had leadership of a band that had an *indefinite contract* with BW. The wanna-be peacock had a long time friendship with BW's ex-significant other. BW handed the decrepit peacock an *indefinite contract* in return for juicing BW's ex on to a television show. As I mentioned a trillion times before, it is all about *politics and money* in this greedy town. The decrepit peacock turned buzzard had a minimal appearance at BW's lounge. The old sagging buzzard enjoyed the company of the bald peacocks and hired a sex-crazed and pedophiliac musician in the band to be a proxy for the missing buzzard.

The front person of the old sickening buzzard's band, who by the way is not the pedophile, had extraordinary talent. The sultry, stunning and sterling musician held the attention of an audience as if watching the magnificent Aurora Borealis in the northern sky. BW should have had the prize winning musician as the master in charge. More than likely, the band would still be performing at BW's lounge.

The shriveled-up wrinkled peacock has identical business traits as CR. The musician's greedy hands swiped money from the budget at BW's lounge while performing with the Crock-pot peacocks. BW loathed all the rotating musicians and the lack of the moribund buzzard's enthusiasm to incorporate new music material. The sickening buzzard abused the *indefinite contract* and BW sliced it into iddy-biddy pieces. I heard through the musical grapevine that the perishing buzzard married the person with the brain disorder called, "Cerebrosclerosis." Hum? Sounds like a perfect match made in brain diseased and decrepit peacock heaven! *Yuck*!

Remember the front person that looks like a flame burning out of control? The orange and red overweight peacock's disturbed mind will experience cock-eyed delusions that rolling out the red carpet is solely for the peacock to strut its feathers. The self-centered and simmering peacock in a Crock-pot believes the band backing up the peacock is the most sensational musical sensation since the Beatles. What is up with that? In my opinion, John Lennon and Paul McCartney were the most astonishing musical writing duo in the world! The peacock's band sounds as if fledgling peacocks are plucking a stringed instrument found lying on the ground in the peacock coup! The burnt and crispy peacock is in charge of the pecking system and receives most of the bird seeds. Hum? I think I will make plans to visit the Los Angeles Zoo and observe the peacocks in their natural habitat.

GG's favorite all time cocky peacock is the leader of a band at a casino off the strip. The overdressed and displeasing peacock struts its feathers as if resplendent diamonds and pearls are draping off the crest of the peacock. The cocky peacock has limited vocal range. The musicians backing up the jewel crested peacock sound like a band of merry minstrels. The casino airs television commercials of the peacock mimicking jungle moves like *Tarzan* swinging from tree vines. I think the television commercials would be more effectual if Jane and Cheetah were starring in them. After GG's cut of the bird seeds, the cocky peacock leader of the merry minstrels probably receives several bushels of bird seeds.

Experts say that the size of most bird brains is comparable to the size of a pea. Obviously, the invention of "You Bird Brain" came from this discovery and insinuates that someone is lacking in intelligence. I believe peacocks were the first bird species that experts experimented with and that is why they have the name peacock. Do you think the latter name of cock was an after thought?

A scantily feathered peacock is the leader of a band that CR cherishes. This wanna-be sex pot peacock's life-long aspiration is to emulate the seductive mannerisms of classic Hollywood movie stars. I would rather watch the AMC Network and google over Joan Crawford or Susan Hayward. With all the bird seeds this entertainer has accumulated in the last four decades, the superannuated and dilapidated peacock should go under the knife to achieve the appearance of classic movie stars. Hum? I guess CR has a sexual fetish for older bird brain peahens.

Peacocks or peahens must always have a clean and refreshing stage appearance. If not, their appearance could offend the audience. Peahens in the Las Vegas music scene have more subjection to discrimination and scrutinized more freely than their happy-go-lucky peacock counterparts. Hum? Sounds exactly what female actors have to endure in Hollywood!

A casino in Laughlin is home to a hairy peahen. The hirsute peahen looks as if the peahen desperately should receive electrolysis or join a circus side show. Please, can anyone buy this whiskered creature a razor? The wolf-like creature has an endless supply of bird seeds, enough to buy the Schick Razor Company! Unfortunately, hormones go awry in both sexes as the aging process takes over the human body. Can you imagine watching an irritating bearded peahen with too much testosterone and a cocky attitude? I would rather watch the androgynous fellows at the casino on the strip. Hum? Does anyone know if peacocks or peahens "cluck"*? Cluck! Cluck! Cluck!*

Peacocks are extremely unrelenting when it comes to their beloved bird seeds. If other peacocks interfere or disrupt a working peacock's environment, then the inevitable cockfight will happen. Not all cockfights occur between two cocks. On occasion, a peacock and peahen will exchange bitter words.

The casino that employs GG's cocky peacock had an extravaganza in their show room that featured two famous artists. Rumor has it that the two leaders of the band, one peacock and one peahen, were regularly fighting and feathers were flying everywhere. The two front peacocks had zero stage chemistry. The casino executives' concern in sagging ticket sales accelerated the cancellation of the *indefinite contract.*

Most casino lounge bands perform Top-40 music. Their musical repertoire will consist of several different musical styles. A hand full of peacocks and their feathered friends will specialize in one style. As I mentioned before, certain casinos will reserve different nights of the week for a style of music.

Illustrations by Nick San Pedro © 2001

Remember the E.D. I called ST? ST's casino decided to build a music stage outside in the middle of ST's casino and the casino next door. It gets extremely hot and sweaty out in the court yard in the summer. As I mentioned two zillion times before, musicians will perform in the middle of a tornado in 120 degree weather to bring home the precious bird seeds.

Some peacocks prefer living in the country. This life style inspires certain peacocks to sing about the country. ST employs a country peacock to sing in the court yard. The hick peacock is pleasant to the eyes, but lacks stage charisma. I can only handle a few minutes of listening to the same old twangy music about good relationships that have gone bad. The back-up musicians look as if the head peacock befriended Old MacDonald's barn yard critters. No *glitz and glamour* in *this* band! More than likely, the twangy sounding peacock is stingy with the bird seeds.

ST has a music band with an *indefinite contract* performing in the courtyard. This style of music will grind on your nerves as if running your finger nails down a chalk board. *Yuck!* I would rather soak up the sunshine on the sultry beaches of St. Croix and listen to the authentic music of the island. I think the casino executives should shut down the merry-go-round and replace the entertainment with the organ grinder and monkey.

PCL managed to snag an ethnic peacock that was performing at one of BW's casinos. Supposedly, BW signed the ethnic peacock to a six month *indefinite contract*. The ethnic peacock is a back-up singer for an ethnic super star singing sensation. One of the musicians in the super star's band has been a staple in the Las Vegas lounge scene for decades. The musician is now a huge time musical director for an extravaganza show at one of the strip casinos. The super star produces the extravaganza show and has close ties with the casino.

The musician and BW have known each other for years. The musician struck up a deal with BW to hire the ethnic peacock and the musician formed a band to back up the ethnic peacock. The deal went sour. BW sliced the *indefinite contract* in to iddy-biddy pieces. PCL came into the picture and showcased the ethnic peacock at one of BW's casinos. PCL invited several Entertainment Directors from other casinos to view the ethnic peacock for future work. Guess what? The place was empty! A few Entertainment Directors managed to drag their gold plated bodies to the show case. At the end of the show, PCL was hanging from a peacock feather off the lounge chandelier.

The ethnic peacock lacked originality. Unfortunately, the monotonous ethnic peacock's show consisted of the same musical songs and choreography of the super star's stage show. More than likely, the E.D.s smelled the similarities and had no interest in booking the ethnic peacock. Hum? I guess the ethnic peacock is not living "La Vida Loca."

One of the back-up musicians for the ethnic peacock is the leader of a band that has an *indefinite contract* at ST's casino. The peacock is not a front person. The ostentatious peacock's attitude reeks of arrogance. The phony peacock's physical appearance looks as if someone rummaged through an old house attic and found a scraggly Troll Doll with a long-haired ponytail. The phony ponytailed peacock should be a guest on the *Jenny Jones Show* and receive a make-over!

Peacocks come in all shapes, sizes, and ages. Las Vegas is about the only city that does not discriminate against the age of entertainers. Entertainers perform well into their late seventies and some peacocks look in their eighties. I think it is just peachy-keen that these entertainers still have the energy to perform. Hum? Do you think they incorporate Geritol and Ensure in their diet?

LL's lounge is home to an elderly peacock entertainer who has been performing in Vegas for five decades. The band members desperately should change their outdated stage costumes and incorporate the colors of a peacock. The front peacock entertainer looks as if constipated for weeks and should drink some prune juice to clean out the same old foul matter that litters the stage. No *glitz and glamour* in *this* band! This is one extremely burnt-out and haggard band. Retirement and relaxation come with the Golden Years. Twenty years from now, this band will still be performing at LL's lounge dressed in skeleton costumes at a Holloween party. More than likely, LL will charge customers a fee for broomstick rides.

LL's lounge plays host to yet another elderly peacock. This is one sexually twisted and confused cow polk. Hum? The country peacock must prefer the smell of cow manure. That would explain why the twangy peacock's stage show stinks! The old coot cross-dresses and incorporates a sexual gadget that is long enough to wrap around LL's broomstick for days. What female in her right state of mind would get sexually aroused by this elephantine piece of plaster? I can think of only one and that would have been Catherine the Great! The old horse wrangler has more than enough bird seeds to buy an assortment of comfortable fitting phallic symbols. The musicians backing up the non-endowed peacock sounds as if cows have stampeded a pasture of month old cow manure. *Pew!*

BW's ex-significant other is an elderly and decaying peacock that works consistently at BW's casinos. Talking about politics and favoritism! BW is notorious for booking the anorexic leather-faced and drug infested peacock. I heard that BW snags the brittle-boned peacock's weekly paycheck. The repulsive peacock has zero talent and the music sounds as if vultures are picking the remains off a peacock carcass. Unfortunately, BW's business savoir-faire is unfair to musicians who deserve the work. I seriously doubt that the entertainment politics in Vegas will change any time soon.

The predominate color of a peacock is blue. Unfortunately, a dilapidated peacock sings about the color blue and the discolored peacock clucks its feathers all over Las Vegas. The fossilized and gray feathered creature performs one night stands at certain casino lounges that cater to this style of music. BW hires the aging blue peacock for the blues night at the casino where the yellow haired scarecrow performs.

The overweight peacock works consistently. The broken down peacock's voice sounds as if the singer ate sand paper and swallowed Lysol to wash down the sand paper. The appearance of the destitute peacock looks as if a homeless person is wearing the same torn and battered clothes for several years. One of the bad batch of witch's brew's significant other is a musician in the old coot's band. The musician looks as if a young kid watched too many *Scooby Doo* cartoons and grew up to look like Shaggy.

Illustrations by Nick San Pedro © 2001

I think I know what all of you are thinking? How does this shamble-looking peacock perform without the *glitz and glamour?* The answer is simple. The aging peacock is a big fish in a small pond. Hum? Do you think peacocks know how to swim? I heard through the peacock musical feather vine, that this peacock's not well liked with the viewing audience and bought a night club to entertain all the lonely peacocks. Unfortunately, only an infinitesimal amount of blues entertainers performs in Las Vegas. The decaying peacock has made a killing with the bird seeds. The aging peacock has several tons of bird seeds to buy the Peacock Coup at the Los Angeles Zoo!

Las Vegas is thirsty for great blues performers. The front person of the old dying buzzard's band had the blues engraved in their soul and the audience felt every note of a song the entertainer performed. As I mentioned before, E.D.s are not privy to good music and great entertainers. Most E.D.s are habitually lazy and refused to hire great entertainers. E.D.s are snug in their comfort zone and it is convenient for them to book the same old pan fried entertainers.

The most pungent and foul smelling peacock in Las Vegas is MC. The dysmorphic and dissymmetric peacock will always exist as the leader of the bad batch of witch's brew and the toothless corn stalk band. The misogynist peacock's forte is spewing out disparaging comments about the opposite sex. The dystonic peacock's significant other must experience dyspareunia while sharing intimate moments with the homely peacock! *Yuck!* You might find a video in cyber space of these two idiosyncratic freaks in a cumbersome position! Hum? How would a bony peacock and a petite Christmas tree "mate"? I really need to visit the Los Angeles Zoo and pay special attention to the mating rituals of peacocks!

Non-musical peacocks are an extenuation of a peacock's stage presentation. They are stage hands. They exist so peacocks do not have to dirty their hands.

Most casinos employ sound technicians. I personally have not worked with any female sound technicians. I do not know if Vegas has any female sound technicians. One thing I do know, BW's casinos have the most egotistical and horrifying sound technicians in Vegas! One sound technician looks as if a Sperm Whale ate three tons of Herring Fish and beached its self to digest the fish. The sound technician's ego is enormous as three beached whales. The Cetacean should go back to school and learn how to run sound. A young kid could run sound better than this blubbering idiot! Hum? I wonder if Sea World is looking for a new Cetacean that weighs three tons?

A few years ago, BW employed a sound technician that was notorious for demanding kickbacks from musicians. BW had no idea that the con artist was ripping off the entertainment acts. The old sickening buzzard supposedly handed over two hundred dollars a week to the wanna-be cockroach. One musician had enough of the money hungry thief and reported the thief's wrong doings to the corporate executives. The casino executives sprayed pesticide on the wanna-be cockroach and gave the wanna-be cockroach walking papers. The wanna-be cockroach found a new dwelling to conduct the same bad business. Hum? I wonder if the wanna-be cockroach and CR attended the same school when they were fledgling cockroaches?

The study of Peacockism is a fascinating and mind boggling subject. Las Vegas is the only city in the world that offers this subject at the prodigious Peacock Institute of Pheasantry. As you all know, the words Peacockism and Pheasantry do not exist. It is just a spoof on words. The students that I just mentioned graduated with honors. All of them received an extra special award in Attendance and Diligence. Unfortunately, there is a waiting list three thousand feathers long of future peacocks to attend this college. If you decide to enroll, make sure you have plenty of bird seeds and patience. The peacocks that rule the music roost in Vegas have no plans to retire their feathers any time soon.

TEN

BACK-UP MUSICIANS

Some peacocks' back-up musicians have their share of personal and business dilemmas. If a musician has a gambling addiction, the problem could jeopardize the musician's livelihood and personal life. It is not a wise decision to move to Las Vegas if you have an addictive personality. I have seen numerous musicians donate all of their musical equipment to pawn shops. Some musicians' marriages and relationships have disintegrated to a pile of ashes over problem gambling. Why do you think Las Vegas has the grand nick name of "Sin City"? Las Vegas will suck you into a vortex of financial despair if you are weak-minded.

Las Vegas is home to a long-beaked musician who is famous for a dangerous gambling addiction. Unfortunately, the musician is in a co-dependent relationship that fuels the fire to continue gambling. In this relationship, both parties are musicians. On one occasion, the musician's significant other's musical equipment took a ride to the pawn shop. The significant other was out-of-town and the grotesque musician went on a gambling spree. What a disgusting mess!

The slimy musician played with the bad batch of witch's brew. The insanely addicted musician begged for financial help from the band members. Only one band

72

member had the finances to bail the addictive jester's significant other's equipment out of the pawn shop. The kind hearted musician continued to help the hypocritical musician with returned visits to the pawn shops. The kind hearted musician realized the diseased musician's addiction was interfering with the professional performance of the band.

The compassionate musician informed MC of the musician's disgusting gambling problem. MC had no idea of the sleazy musician's gambling addiction and set up a meeting with the other band members. Well, guess what? MC fired the generous musician and kept the diseased addicted musician. Do you want to know why? The other brainless band members were close friends with the diseased musician and thought the sickly musician was more valuable than the kind hearted musician. The stone cold truth is, the kind hearted musician was more talented than all the members in the band and was a musical threat to MC.

Is there any "MUSICIAL JUSTICE" in the world? No! Hard working musicians always finish last! The back stabbing gargoyles kissed MC's hideous ass to keep their jobs. I bet MC's backside smells like peacock manure! *Pew!* If the gargoyles were such close buddies of the trouble maker musician, why didn't they come to the financial rescue of the alcoholic and indigent musician? Hum? I guess birds of the same *do* feather flock together!

Remember the pedophiliac musician that was a proxy for the old perishing buzzard? This musician has a severe addiction to gambling. The musician spends every dollar and every cent on gambling. The strung out musician's obsession with placing the next bet interfered with the musician's professionalism while at work.

Here is a story that will knock you off your drum stool. The lounge where the old sickening buzzard's band performed had big screen televisions on the wall next to the music stage. While the addicted musician was performing on stage, the musician would watch the televisions for all the sport scores. The musician would stop performing in a middle of a song and scream when a sports team scored. The audience reaction to this out of control addict was as if watching a delirious patient escaping from an insane asylum.

I have several sick stories about this deranged and sex-crazed musician. The ingratiating musician would desperately try to pick up on the opposite sex. The musician's method of sexual operation lacked finesse. I heard that the over-sexed musician embarrassed the opposite sex by asking them if they shaved their genital area. The audacity of this musician to ask strangers intimate sexual questions, is way out in left field! I can think of other pick up lines that would be more influential and seductive. Do not say a word. Silence is golden. Just show the person your wallet stuffed with money. Now, that is what you would call a perfect score!

Usually, the sex-demented musician was in charge of hiring musicians to fill in for the absent expiring buzzard. The choice of musicians looks as if Santa Claus left all the rejected and malfunctioning toys under the over-sexed musician's fake Christmas tree. The perverted musician decided to bring the faulty toys to work and try them out on stage. What a disaster! All the musicians were horrible.

One musician looked as if someone chopped off the head eggs. The egg head musician also had a menacing gambling problem. Between these two addicted gamblers, the band never started playing on time. The band was famous for starting their performances fifteen to twenty minutes late.

Here is another story that is a humdinger. This infantile acting musician came to work in a football jersey and a helmet. The musician had a slew of tiny footballs sprawled all over the stage. I guess the musician's life-long dream is to be a quarterback. The old sickening buzzard did not show any concern for the musician's unprofessional behavior. The old buzzard was never at the lounge to supervise the band. I heard through the musical note vine, that most of the bartenders and waitresses loathed the toddler musician. The musician's imbecile behavior offended the audience. Would you want to watch this lunatic musician perform? The lounge clientele diminished over time and so did the old buzzard's *indefinite contract*.

This next story revolves around a close friend of mine. My friend is one of the sweetest people you could ever meet. Unfortunately, the gambling vortex invaded my friend's life and the spiraling destruction left my friend almost penniless. In one year alone, my friend won a whopping one hundred thousand dollars. The addictive thrill of winning accelerated my friend into a manic gambling spree. The manic musician was kind enough to give back the casinos all the money the musician won, plus several thousand dollars on top of the winnings. As I mentioned before, Las Vegas has a dark maniacal side that will destroy and demolish your life if you have an addictive personality.

Most musicians and peacocks are constant complainers. They belong to the "Whiners Club" of Las Vegas. Musicians resemble babies with colic, habitually crying and never satisfied. They always whine when they are out of work as well as whine when they have work. Would all of you like to hear some of the whiners' complaints?

1. "The gig is too many hours!"

2. "I do not like the sound system!"

3. "I cannot hear the monitors!"

4. "I cannot hear the reverb in the monitors!"

5. "I need to see a contract!"

6. "How many days is the gig?"

7. "Do we have to rehearse?"

8. "Do we get free bottled water?"

9. "Is the gig an *indefinite contract?*"

If the leader of the band prefers musicians on a certain instrument, they complain if they cannot have the spot light. They would be better off at home with a bottle in their mouth and a diaper on their derrieres. Most of these cry babies are aware that CR and MC have sole ownership of *lounge contracts* and *indefinite contracts*.

Here is a quick story that is apart from the music business. I feel that I need to stress upon all of you how living in Las Vegas can destroy the typical family.

Some casinos in Vegas have movie theaters and offer baby-sitting services while you are watching your favorite flick. Unfortunately, some people will pawn off their children for a couple of hours to gamble. Not a good idea!

A close friend of mine and my friend's significant other was watching a movie at one of the local casinos. When exiting the movie, they noticed a big commotion in front of the baby-sitting service area. Many uniformed police officers and hotel security were swarming the front desk of the baby-sitting service. Out of curiosity, my friend decided to get a closer look at all the turmoil. My friend spotted someone that they knew in the middle of all the commotion. The unfortunate friend was sucked into the gambling vortex and could not afford to bail the children out of the baby-sitting service. The service called the police and the unfortunate person was about to take an unpleasant ride to the police station for child endangerment. My friend came to the financial rescue of the penniless parent and bailed the children out of the baby-sitting service.

What ever happen to the happy family picnics at the neighborhood park? You will not find many parks in *this* city! Big casino corporations monopolize Las Vegas real estate. This city's number one priority is building the next casino. Casino executives want your money and they could care less if a family disintegrates over gambling. The Mayor of Las Vegas is doing a superb job of revitalizing down town Vegas and offering different venues for tourists and locals to enjoy instead of gambling.

ELEVEN

TWO, THREE AND FOUR WALLING CONTRACTS

In the good old days, Vegas entertainment had a protective fortress guarded by the Mafia. Vegas was a musician's nirvana of endless gigs. The Mafia owned and operated several casinos. In a way, they had their own musicians' union. Today, greedy corporations own and operate casinos in Las Vegas. The days of making one hundred thousand dollars a week is just a memory. The current day method of paychecks comes in the form of *two-walling, three-walling,* and *four-walling contracts.* It is the responsibility of entertainers to sell tickets, not the casino. Now you know why show ticket prices are out of this world and in a galaxy of their own! An entertainer's livelihood survives solely off ticket sales. Casino executives viciously refuse to pick up the entire paycheck of an entertainer.

Two-walling simply means a ratio of 50-50. The casino picks up half of the entertainer's paycheck. Most of the extravaganzas on the strip are working under some form of *two, three*, or *four-walling contract*. Entertainers pay the casino executives to lease the room in which they are performing. It is a rare occasion if the casino pays an entertainer a flat salary. I have heard that a famous comedian had a *two-walling contract* at a casino on the strip. The comedian ticket sales were outstanding, so the casino executives decided to pay the comedian a straight salary. All of us entertainers in Vegas wish we had it that easy.

Three-walling is a ratio of 80-20 or some other ratio in favor of the casino. Again, the entertainers have to pay rent on the room they are using to perform. If an entertainer is struggling with ticket sales, the musicians backing up the entertainer are lucky if they receive a paycheck. If the entertainer fails to pay rent, the casino has no choice but to fire the entertainer. Unfortunately, entertainers pay a heavy price for maintaining *glitz and glamour* in Vegas.

This miserable way of conducting business gets worse. *Four-walling* ratio is 100-0 in total favor of the casino. The entertainer's income is strictly off tickets sales. If entertainers are struggling with ticket sales, how in the heck can they afford to pay rent? That is why there is so much turnover of entertainers in Vegas. In the future, the *glitz and glamour* will have an intrusive way of getting more expensive for Las Vegas entertainers.

Last summer, Robert Goulet signed a *four-walling contract* with a huge casino on the strip. Would all of you like to take a guess what Goulet paid the casino executives per night for rent? How about a whopping fifteen thousand dollars per night! *Ouch!* Goulet said it was the most stupid and ridiculous business contract he ever signed. Unfortunately, Goulet canceled his *indefinite contract* with the casino.

I heard that the same casino is *four-walling* a magician. This fabulous magician sells roughly seventy-five thousand dollars a week in ticket sales. By the time everyone involved in the show and the casino executives get their share of the money, the magician brings home fifteen to eighteen thousand dollars a week. All of you are probably thinking that it is superior pay for one week. Considering all the exhaustive work the magician puts into the show, the money is infinitesimal. It is the entertainers' responsibility to make sure their shows are top notch, no matter how much they cost.

Another strip casino employed an impersonator with a *four-walling contract* that was having a difficult time selling tickets. The casino executives fired the impersonator and decided to replace the act with a famous singing star that has been in the business for decades. Casino executives are relying on this super star to bring in the money. Good Luck! Ticket prices have gone straight though the galaxy and are neighbors of the planet, Uranus!

This type of bureaucratic business is not just indigenous to strip casinos. Casino show rooms that are disseminated through out Vegas usually practice some form of the *two, three or four-walling* format. Casino executives blanket themselves financially with keeping up with the casino Jones's. All the mega casinos are in competition with each other to build the biggest casino. Almost every casino is under some form of construction. The *two, three and four-walling* format allows a little extra money for them to go on spending sprees to upgrade their casinos. Do you really think the Grinches would take a cut in their pay? All of them would rather lay-off their minimum wage workers, just to have the cushy padding of money in their back pockets. Speaking of minimum wage, I highly suggest that you tip dealers, especially if you are on a winning streak.

The rubber-legged souls stand for hours and have to endure verbal backlash from all the drunken gambling morons.

I seriously doubt that casino lounges will adopt *two, three or four-walling* policies. All lounge entertainment serves as a free listening gallery for the tourists and gamblers. As I mentioned numerous times before, most Las Vegas lounge entertainment is appalling and atrocious. Hum? Casino executives should sell tickets to their lounges. Any tourist in their right state of mind would never buy these tickets and then CR's Cockroach Productions would go out of business. YAHOOOOO! Every musician in Vegas would have a "CR IS GOING OUT OF BUSINESS PARTY" with a dart-throwing contest and a picture of CR as the target. CR is very tiny, so you need to have 20-20 vision to hit the bull's eye. I would also use a picture of MC as the target. I would experience absolute and mind thrilling satisfaction throwing a dart at MC's repulsive and disfigured face.

TWELVE

BUSINESS CONVENTIONS

Illustrations by Nick San Pedro © 2001

Las Vegas is a Mecca for every type of business convention. This city plays host to the annual Pornography convention extravaganza. Sin City becomes submerged in a sea of sex with every XXX rated movie star and all the new sexual gadgets that will dazzle your sexual pleasures. If you are a faithful worshiper of sexual hedonism, this convention most definitely would serve as your erotic playground.

Most all conventions have live music entertainment or impersonators. Entertainment is an audio backdrop for the conventioneers. Unfortunately, CR provides most of the entertainment. CR is one busy little thieving cockroach that is getting the last laugh on everyone who conducts business with the sticky insect.

CEOs love Las Vegas for all the obvious reasons. Las Vegas is the city to promote their business products and mingle with potential buyers to enhance the financial future of their companies. The Las Vegas Convention Center is the main show room for big name companies. All the famous high-tech companies reserve this colossal hub for their conventions. Usually, most casinos have a convention room to host other types of conventions. Conventions are a huge source of money for casinos.

Knowledge is the number one quality that CEOs pride themselves on and that is why their companies are successful. Aim for excellence and the sky's the limit.

Now, this is when I get to burst CEO's pecuniary balloons. I get to inform CEOs how CR is blatantly ripping off their business and insulting their business intelligence. When they hire entertainment acts from CR's Cockroach Productions, they are paying up the wah-zoo and being raked over the money sizzling coals. They might as well

L.S. Baker

throw the money they allocate for entertainment for conventions into the barbecue pit and listen to the sounds of money disappearing. So, listen up high powered CEOs! I have something to tell you! Knowledge is powerful!

Illustrations by Nick San Pedro © 2001

I will now throw out some legal tender figures that CR demands for a typical convention. Depending on the financial status of the company, CR will demand all the gold bars that a company is willing to pay. Usually, the amount is between ten and fifteen thousand dollars. I have heard that CR's price will go as high as twenty thousand dollars. This amount of money shakes off the Musical Richter Scale! Since CR and MC have their own musical convention band, they hog out on the high paying conventions. CR's band even hides behind sequenced music tracks.

Why would you want to pay an astronomical price for fake music? Companies would be better off hiring a DJ for a fraction of CR's ridiculous price.

Most of CR's convention entertainment acts incorporate sequenced music tracks. Most conventioneers probably think the musical entertainment sounds great. What a misconception! You might as well stick a CD in the CD player and pump up the volume... Do a little dance... Make a little love... Get down tonight! Hum? I have a superb idea for convention entertainment. I think it would be a great gimmick to have beautiful females splashing their ethereal bodies in a bubbling hot tub while promoting your business products. Now, that is entertainment!

Here is the convention booth's financial truth. When you contract entertainment from CR, a huge portion of the money you pay CR never lands in the musician's hand. CR takes a healthy bite off the silver platter and the remaining crumbs add up to three to five thousand dollars per band. CR even takes fifteen or twenty percent off the three to five thousand dollars. The lining of CR's cockroach designer clothes has secret compartments stuffed with five to fifteen thousand dollars per band. Why would you want to contribute all that hard earned money to CR's get rich quick scam? If your company is looking for a financial write-off, donate it to a legitimate charity. Las Vegas homeless shelters are in dire need of food and money. CR certainly would not contribute any money to any worthy cause. If CR was to donate fifteen percent of CR's yearly income to the homeless, they would be able to have food and shelter for five years. Hum? Do you think the IRS would like a contribution from CR?

The only way to eliminate CR's scam is to eliminate CR. You must refuse to pay the price CR demands for convention entertainment. You should only pay three to five thousand dollars for the entertainment. This way, CR would only pocket the fifteen or twenty percent. If CR throws a temper tantrum and refuses to contract a band at five thousand dollars, go elsewhere. Las Vegas has plenty of musical agencies that will accommodate you for affordable entertainment. More than likely, you will get acceptable entertainment. You might want to contact GG's classy act agency for entertainment. GG might demand seven to eight thousand dollars, but at least you would get *glitz and glamour*.

THIRTEEN

CLEANING UP THE ENTERTAINMNET POLITICS

The only possible solution to clean up the dirty musical politics in Vegas, is to boycott CR and the other sleaze slice agents. Musicians can book their bands without agents. I seriously doubt that this major overhaul will occur anytime soon, but you can get the cat's meowing started by contacting legitimate agencies for entertainment. I feel the solution is in the hands of the Mayor of Las Vegas. The Mayor has the power to investigate CR's shady scams. All parties involved would benefit, especially casino executives, since they have the authority of allocating casino entertainment budgets. I do not think they would appreciate their Entertainment Directors eagerness to extort entertainment money and kickback money from CR.

Another possible solution that could work, is if a reputable big time entertainment agency moves to Las Vegas and takes full control of supplying all the lounge entertainment to all the casinos. I wonder if any multi-millionaire entrepreneurs would like to take on a new business endeavor? It would be a win-win situation for all parties involved. The entertainment would be of stellar quality and the entertainers could finally get an honest paycheck. Casino executives could eliminate the position of most of the annoying lounge Entertainment Directors and concentrate directing that money to accommodate their customers' demands. Moreover, casino executives could up the pay for their diligent working dealers.

FOURTEEN

LAS VEGAS IDENTITY CRISIS

Las Vegas as a city and Las Vegas casino entertainment are experiencing a massive identity crisis. Casino executives are fervently exploiting their mega casinos as an adult style Disneyland with child-like theme amenities. What is up with that? Casino executives want more money, of course! Hum? Vegas casinos are probably planning to build an amusement park ride that is similar to Disneyland's *Its A Small Small World* with Black Jack tables as the transport buggies. More than likely, you would have to pay a one hundred dollar table minimum.

In the good old days, Vegas was an adult playground and children were *persona non grata*. The city of lights was an endless reservation for adults to indulge themselves in the frenzy of stellar entertainers and the old nostalgia type gambling. I do not know if some of you are a lover of the one arm bandit, but I despise the new slot machine technology. Almost every television show and cartoon is now a theme of most slot machines. I guess casino executives want adults to recapture their childhood and to live it vicariously through infant theme machines? It is just a matter of time before cocktail waitresses start wearing *Teletubbies* costumes.

Everything in a casino is a subliminal money-making gimmick. Well, why not? People come to Las Vegas to experience the bigger than life ambience of mental stimulation regardless the price on the price tag. Should there be an endless price on pleasure and relaxation when you visit Las Vegas? The casino executives are counting on your vulnerability and hope you succumb to the high price of *glitz and glamour*.

Casinoville will always attract tourists. Thousands of people move to Las Vegas monthly, in search of solid and secure employment. Entertainers flock here in droves in hopes of cashing in on the spot light glory. New housing developments spring up as fast as losing your money at a casino. Casino implosions are commonplace and transposed with monstrous mega resorts. The sparkling lights on the famous strip do not have a dimmer switch. It would be a cold day in hell before anyone pulls the plug on the sparkling lights.

Who would ever think that a small town in a desert would grow up to be such a roaring metropolis? I believe gregarious Mafia mobster Bugsy Seigel had such a vision. If Bugsy could only see Las Vegas today, he would be one proud papa. Frank Sinatra and his musical comrades engraved an unprecedented one-of-a-kind entertainment magic that present day entertainers wish they could recapture. Las Vegas will never experience and feel the euphoria of the good old days. The only way to sum up the number one party town, is though the words of The King. "VIVA LAS VEGAS!"

ABOUT THE AUTHOR

L. S. Baker is a musician that currently resides and performs in Las Vegas. International appearances include Europe and other countries.

Printed in the United States
6377